World Geography
Student Workbook

by
Marcel Lewinski

Wieser Educational

30281 Esperanza
Rancho Santa Margarita, CA 92688-2130
1(800) 880-4433 ♦ Fax (800) 949-0209

www.wieser-ed.com ♦ Email info@wieser-ed.com

Printed in the United States of America

ISBN 0-7854-2439-3

Product Number 91503

A 0 9 8 7 6

Table of Contents

U.S. Trivia

Directions: Circle the letter of the correct answer.

1) North America is
   a. a country.
   b. a continent.
   c. an ocean.
   d. a city.

2) The equator is
   a. an imaginary line that goes around the middle of Earth.
   b. a fixed point at zero degrees longitude.
   c. a line that shows how far east or west a place is.
   d. a line that forms the border between North America and South America.

3) The Prime Meridian runs through
   a. Washington, D.C.
   b. Greenwich, England.
   c. Baltimore, Maryland.
   d. Denver, Colorado.

4) The first region to build industries was
   a. the West.
   b. the South.
   c. the Northeast.
   d. the Midwest.

5) The South contains
   a. 14 states.
   b. 12 states.
   c. 13 states.
   d. 16 states.

6) The South attracts factory owners
   a. because of its mild climate and lower cost of labor.
   b. because it has the oldest factories in the country.
   c. because it is a center for the banking industry.
   d. because a lot of people live there.

7) Much of the Midwest region is
   a. a dense forest.
   b. a large plain.
   c. a dry desert.
   d. an island.

8) Many midwestern farmers grow
   a. grasses and mosses.
   b. cotton and rice.
   c. corn and soybeans.
   d. oranges and pineapples.

9) The largest of the four regions in the United States is
   a. the South.
   b. the Northeast.
   c. the Midwest.
   d. the West.

10) An area in which few or no people live is a
    a. plain.
    b. desert.
    c. subregion.
    d. suburb.

All About the United States

Directions: Write the correct word from the Word Bank to complete
these sentences.

Word Bank				
Prime Meridian	seven	California	regions	Northeast
western	cotton	Mexico	latitude	Midwest

1) _____ borders the United States on the south.

2) There are _____ continents on Earth.

3) Geographers use _____ to describe how far north or south of the
equator a place is.

4) Longitude is measured from the _____.

5) Geographers define _____ according to their physical, economic,
and historic features.

6) The capital of the United States is in the _____ region.

7) At one time, the South grew much of the world's _____.

8) The _____ is called America's breadbasket.

9) The Rocky Mountains are in the _____ region.

10) Most of the people in the western region live in _____.

Physical Feature Match-Up

Directions: Match the words in column 1 with their meanings in
column 2. Write the letter on the line.

_____ **1)** delta

_____ **2)** basin

_____ **3)** weather

_____ **4)** steppe climate

_____ **5)** glacier

_____ **6)** tributary

_____ **7)** highland climate

_____ **8)** leeward

_____ **9)** precipitation

_____ **10)** sea level

_____ **11)** windward

_____ **12)** Mediterranean climate

_____ **13)** climate

_____ **14)** subtropical climate

_____ **15)** Tropic of Cancer

a. large, slow-moving sheet of ice

b. imaginary line that lies 23.5 degrees north
of the equator

c. side from which the wind is blowing

d. area of rich land at the mouth of a river

e. level at the surface of the ocean

f. climate with very hot summers and very
cold winters, with little precipitation

g. low area of land surrounded by higher land

h. average of weather conditions over a
period of time

i. climate with hot and humid summers and
mild winters

j. climate with mild, wet winters and hot, dry
summers

k. smaller river that flows into a bigger one

l. how much rain, snow, or sleet falls from
the sky

m. condition of the air at a given time or place

n. side away from the wind

o. varying climate of a mountainous area

Culture in the United States

Directions: Write the answers to these questions using complete sentences.

1) What is culture?

   _____

2) How do cultures change?

   _____

   _____

3) What are two branches of Christianity?

   _____

4) What are two most widely spoken languages in the United States?

   _____

5) What is a rural area?

   _____

6) Where do most citizens of the United States live?

   _____

7) What is a megalopolis?

   _____

8) How did changes in transportation affect the development of cities in the United States?

   _____

   _____

9) Why is Chicago a railroad center?

   _____

10) What two population trends affect the United States today?

   _____

   _____

Environmental Facts

Directions: Read each sentence. Write *T* if the statement is *true* or *F* if
it is *false*.

_____   **1)** The second largest country in the world is the United States.

_____   **2)** Rich natural resources are one reason U.S. citizens live better than people in many other countries.

_____   **3)** Forests are a renewable resource.

_____   **4)** Oceans provide pulp to make paper.

_____   **5)** The U.S. owns all of the known coal deposits on Earth.

_____   **6)** Most coal mining in the U.S. takes place in the Rocky Mountains.

_____   **7)** Oil and natural gas are found along the Texas and Louisiana coasts of the Gulf of Mexico.

_____   **8)** Many important minerals have been discovered on the midwestern plains.

_____   **9)** Using natural resources in the U.S. was more expensive than using imports.

_____   **10)** Steel is made from iron ore and coal.

_____   **11)** Pittsburgh, Pennsylvania, is the home of the automobile industry.

_____   **12)** Most workers in the United States are involved in manufacturing.

_____   **13)** A clothing store is an example of a service industry.

_____   **14)** Air pollution is a common problem in rural areas.

_____   **15)** Industries can be a source of water pollution.

The Political Regions of Canada

Directions: Fill in the blanks to complete the list of Canada's
provinces and territories.

Provinces   **Description**

1) The Maritime Provinces

    a. _____   Grand Banks off its coast, fishing

    New Brunswick

    Nova Scotia

    Prince Edward Island

    b. _____   island, has flat farmland

2) **c.** _____   largest province, center of manufacturing

3) **d.** _____   hub of industry

4) The Prairie Provinces

    Manitoba

    e. _____   mostly agricultural

    f. _____   gas, oil, tourism

5) **g.** _____   high mountains, thick forests,
salmon, Pacific port

Territories

6) The Arctic North

    h. _____ Territory

    i. _____   home of Inuit

    j. _____ Territories

Physical Features Match-Up

Directions: Match each term on the left with the correct description
on the right. Write the correct letter on the line.

_____ **1)** glaciers

_____ **2)** geologist

_____ **3)** Cordillera

_____ **4)** Coast Mountains

_____ **5)** Mt. Logan

_____ **6)** Ellesmere

_____ **7)** subarctic climate

_____ **8)** Great Lakes

_____ **9)** St. Lawrence lowlands

_____ **10)** permafrost

_____ **11)** continental climate

_____ **12)** Chinook

_____ **13)** landlocked

_____ **14)** maritime climate

_____ **15)** humid continental climate

a. area with heavy population and industry

b. western mountain range

c. ground that is always frozen

d. Spanish word for mountain range

e. a dry, hot wind off the Rocky Mountains

f. tallest peak in the St. Elias Mountains

g. rainy climate on Canada's West Coast

h. surrounded by land on all sides

i. ice that shaped Canada's landscape

j. mildest Canadian climate with four seasons

k. scientist who studies physical features of Earth

l. cold, dry climate

m. large island in northern Canada

n. huge lakes between the U.S. and Canada

o. climate with short, warm summers and long
winters

Canada's People

Directions: Write the answers to these questions using complete sentences.

1) Why is the Inuit way of life changing?

_____

_____

_____

2) How have Europe and Asia contributed to Canadian culture?

_____

_____

_____

3) What makes Toronto such an important Canadian city?

_____

_____

_____

4) What three important trends affect Canada today?

_____

_____

_____

5) What conflict over language and government exists in Quebec today?

_____

_____

_____

Canada's Economy and Environment True or False

Directions: Read each sentence. Write *T* if the statement is *true* or *F* if
it is *false*.

_____ **1)** Canada has only a few natural resources.

_____ **2)** Canada has a booming commercial fishing industry.

_____ **3)** One-fourth of Canada's land is covered by forests.

_____ **4)** Canada is the world leader in oil and gas production.

_____ **5)** Canada's single largest export is products made from wood.

_____ **6)** Canada exports lumber only to Asia.

_____ **7)** Most Canadians work in mining or agriculture.

_____ **8)** Farm products make up 3 percent of the Canadian economy.

_____ **9)** The tourism, banking, and restaurant industries employ the most Canadians.

_____ **10)** Canada has less trouble getting rid of its garbage than the U.S. does.

_____ **11)** Soil erosion has become a problem because of poor mining methods.

_____ **12)** Canada needs to find ways to renew forests lost to logging.

_____ **13)** Wetlands are needed to prevent the land from flooding.

_____ **14)** Draining wetlands creates more homes for birds.

_____ **15)** Acid rain is only a threat to wildlife, not people or buildings.

Exploring Mexico

Directions: Complete the paragraphs below. Write the correct word
from the Word Bank to complete each sentence.

Word Bank		
United States	Central Plateau	irrigation
isthmus	coastal plains	jungle
desert	Yucatán	Sonoran
Mexico City	plate tectonics	corn
triangular	Valley of Mexico	peninsula

Mexico is bordered on the north by the **1)** _____ and on the south by

Central American countries. It is **2)** _____ in shape. The narrowest part is an

3) _____, a narrow strip of land that is only 134 miles wide.

The largest physical region is the **4)** _____, an area of level highland. In

the north it is dry and crops are watered by **5)** _____; in the south it is rainy and

farmers grow **6)** _____. In the heart of this rich southern region lies the

7) _____, lowlands between mountains. The capital of Mexico,

8) _____, is located here. **9)** _____, or movement of Earth's

giant plates, cause earthquakes in this region and form mountains.

The **10)** _____ form a rim around Mexico's Central Plateau and

mountains. These strips of land are dry in the north and covered with **11)** _____

in the south.

Two other physical regions of Mexico are the northwestern **12)** _____

region and the **13)** _____ Peninsula. Two deserts are

14) _____ and Baja California. A **15)** _____ is a strip of land

surrounded by water on three sides.

Mexico's Mountains and Climate

Directions: Read each sentence. Write *T* if the statement is *true* or *F* if
it is *false*.

_____ 1) The main physical feature of Mexico is its mountains.

_____ 2) The Sierra Madre is a series of mountain ranges in Mexico.

_____ 3) Only deciduous trees grow on Mexico's mountains.

_____ 4) The tallest mountain in Mexico is Popocatépetl.

_____ 5) Pico de Orizaba is the volcano that erupted most recently in Mexico.

_____ 6) Mexico's coastline is famous for its beautiful beaches.

_____ 7) The Río Bravo is a large lake in Mexico.

_____ 8) Because Mexico is so flat, it does not have many river systems.

_____ 9) A steppe climate is very dry and always hot.

_____ 10) Most of Mexico has a tropical savanna climate.

_____ 11) Altitude is the height a place is above sea level.

_____ 12) High altitudes cause some parts of Mexico to be cool and rainy.

_____ 13) The French gave special names to Mexico's three altitudinal zones.

_____ 14) Tierra caliente describes higher altitudes that are moderate.

_____ 15) Tierra fría refers to the highest altitudes with the coldest temperatures.

The People of Mexico

Directions: Choose the answer that best completes each statement.
Write the letter of the answer on the line.

1) Before Europeans came, the _____ built a
great empire in Yucatán and Guatemala.

    a. mestizos

    b. Mayas

    c. Aztecs

    d. Toltecs

2) The culture of the _____ blends ways of
native and European people.

    a. tamales

    b. Nahuatls

    c. mestizos

    d. Aztecs

3) _____ of the population is descended
from native people.

    a. 10 percent

    b. 15 percent

    c. 30 percent

    d. 75 percent

4) The language spoken in the government,
businesses, and schools is _____.

    a. Spanish

    b. native

    c. Nahuatl

    d. English

5) More than 90 percent of the Mexican
people belong to the _____ Church.

    a. Roman Catholic

    b. Protestant

    c. Toltec

    d. Hindu

6) From 1900 to 2000, the Mexican
population grew from _____.

    a. 5 million to 20 million people

    b. 13 million to 100 million people

    c. 50 million to 200 million people

    d. 50 million to 500 million people

7) Poor farmers who moved to urban areas
seeking a better life are called _____.

    a. mestizos

    b. immigrants

    c. descendants

    d. campesinos

8) Mexico City's slums are _____.

    a. fine places to shop

    b. noisy city markets

    c. poor, overcrowded areas

    d. wealthy trading centers

9) Three Mexican cities, in order from
largest to smallest, are _____.

    a. Vera Cruz, Guadalajara, Tampico

    b. Mexico City, Guadalajara,
Monterrey

    c. Monterrey, Vera Cruz,
Guadalajara

    d. Mexico City, Monterrey,
Acapulco

10) The trend in Mexico, and in much of the
world, is for people to _____.

    a. move out of the cities

    b. move from rural areas to cities

    c. try to avoid working for a living

    d. work in factories

Economy and Environment in Mexico

Directions: Write the answers to these questions using complete sentences.

1) Why is oil so important to Mexico's economy?

_____

2) Why does the government want Mexican farmers to work in manufacturing?

_____

_____

3) In a maquiladora, who does the work and who owns the products that are made?

_____

4) Why is tourism a big industry in Mexico?

_____

_____

5) What happened as a result of the signing of NAFTA?

_____

_____

6) How much of the Mexican population is poor?

_____

7) Which part of the population tends to be poorest?

_____

8) What type of cutbacks has the government been forced to make because of the foreign debt?

_____

_____

9) What are three sources of water pollution in Mexico's rivers?

_____

10) Why is garbage a problem in Mexico City?

_____

Facts About Central America and the Caribbean

Directions: Circle the word(s) in parentheses that best complete(s) each sentence.

1) In the north, Central America borders (Colombia, Mexico).

2) The Antilles are a(n) (archipelago, rimland).

3) Another name for the Greater and Lesser Antilles is the (Bahamas, West Indies).

4) (Jamaica, Hispaniola) is divided into two nations: Haiti and the Dominican Republic.

5) The Bahamas lie farther (south, north) than the rest of the Caribbean islands.

6) Geographers divide Central America and the Caribbean into two (continents, subregions).

7) (Panama, Cuba) is on the mainland of Central America.

8) Most mainland people are (mestizos, African).

9) Many Caribbean islands were once ruled by (the United States, European countries).

10) After conquering the mainland, the Spanish divided the land into (haciendas, cities).

11) (Spanish landlords, Native people and mestizos) did most of the work on haciendas.

12) People who are (dependent, self-sufficient) take care of their own needs without outside help.

13) The Spanish divided the land on the islands into (plantations, haciendas).

14) On a (hacienda, plantation), many crops were grown.

15) Crops that are sold are called (food crops, cash crops).

Physical Features Crossword Puzzle

Directions: Read each clue. Choose a word from the Word Bank to complete the puzzle.

Word Bank				
highland	hurricane	dormant	atolls	rain forests
Nicaragua	mountains	Panama	navigable	geothermal

Across

2) Many islands in the Caribbean are the tops of this kind of volcano.

4) These cover the eastern side of Central America.

7) This tropical storm brings strong winds and heavy rainfall.

8) This country owns and runs the Panama Canal.

9) These nonvolcanic islands are made from the remains of corals.

10) This is the type of climate that mountain areas of Central America have.

Down

1) Some of these are more than 13,000 feet high in Central America.

3) This kind of power comes from the heat of volcanoes.

5) This describes a body of water that is deep enough and wide enough for ships to sail on.

6) This is an important lake in Central America.

Central American and Caribbean Cultures

Directions: Circle the letter of the correct answer.

1) Half the population is native people in
   a. Honduras.
   b. Guatemala.
   c. Costa Rica.
   d. Panama.

2) Central American culture was heavily influenced by
   a. Spain.
   b. France.
   c. England.
   d. Mexico.

3) A large part of the population of Belize is descended from
   a. Europeans.
   b. Mexicans.
   c. Africans.
   d. Americans.

4) A person of mixed European and African descent is a
   a. mulatto.
   b. mestizo.
   c. slave.
   d. citizen.

5) Africans were originally brought to the islands to work as slaves
   a. on haciendas.
   b. on fishing boats.
   c. in large cities.
   d. on sugarcane plantations.

6) The mixture of French and African languages is called
   a. creole.
   b. voodoo.
   c. reggae.
   d. Spanish.

7) Most people in Jamaica and the Bahamas speak
   a. Spanish.
   b. English.
   c. French.
   d. creole.

8) The only country in Central America with a high population density is
   a. Honduras.
   b. Panama.
   c. Guatemala.
   d. El Salvador.

9) Oscar Arias Sánchez was the president of
   a. Nicaragua.
   b. Costa Rica.
   c. the Dominican Republic.
   d. Cuba.

10) The United States controls
   a. Puerto Rico.
   b. Cuba.
   c. Haiti.
   d. Panama.

Environmental Meaning

Directions: Define each of the following words. Then write a sentence
using the word.

1) overdevelopment

Definition: _____

Sentence: _____

_____

2) extinct

Definition: _____

Sentence: _____

_____

3) subsistence farming

Definition: _____

Sentence: _____

_____

4) bauxite

Definition: _____

Sentence: _____

_____

5) tourism

Definition: _____

Sentence: _____

_____

What Do You Know About South America?

Directions: Circle the word(s) that best complete(s) each of the sentences.

1) A large part of South America is (north of the equator, in the Tropics).

2) The equator runs through the countries of Brazil, Colombia, and (Ecuador, Bolivia).

3) The theory that explains how the seven continents formed is called (continental drift, Pangaea).

4) Fossils are molds or parts of ancient (plants and animals, rocks and minerals).

5) The first region to which Europeans came was (Atlantic South America, Caribbean South America).

6) French Guiana is a (territory, country) in South America.

7) A (large plain, rocky mountain range) stretches across Venezuela.

8) The largest country in South America is (Argentina, Brazil).

9) Most Brazilians live in the (western, southeastern) part of the country.

10) The new capital of Brazil is (Brasília, São Paulo).

11) Amazonia covers (much of, very little of) Brazil.

12) The Andes Mountains are (lower, higher) than the Rocky Mountains.

13) The (*Altiplano, campo cerrado*) stretches across Peru and Bolivia.

14) Ecuador, Peru, Bolivia, and Chile are part of (Atlantic South America, Pacific South America).

15) The narrowest country in South America is (Chile, Colombia).

Name _____   Date _____   Period _____

Physical Features of South America

Directions: Read the words in the Word Bank. On the line before each sentence,
write the letter of the correct word(s) to complete each sentence.

Word Bank

a. pampas   **e.** Tierra del Fuego   **i.** tributaries

b. Angel   **f.** Atacama   **j.** plateaus

c. foothill   **g.** Orinoco

d. Rio de la Plata **h.** Patagonia

_____ 1) The Andes Mountains begin at _____.

_____ 2) A _____ is a hill at the base of a mountain range.

_____ 3) The plains of Argentina are called the _____.

_____ 4) There is a large area of lowlands and _____ in Brazil.

_____ 5) The Amazon has over 1,000 _____.

_____ 6) The _____ is important to Argentina, Paraguay, and Uruguay.

_____ 7) The _____ is a major river system in Venezuela.

_____ 8) The world's tallest waterfall is _____ Falls.

_____ 9) The _____ Desert is one of the world's driest deserts.

_____ 10) _____ is a dry, cold area at the southern tip of South America.

The Cultures of South America

Directions: Circle the letter of the correct answer.

1) South America is divided into
   a. five cultural regions.
   b. four cultural regions.
   c. three cultural regions.
   d. two cultural regions.

2) Large parts of Bolivia, Peru, Ecuador, and part of Colombia make up
   a. Euro-America.
   b. Indo-America.
   c. Afro-America.
   d. Pacific America.

3) Native people of Indo-America
   a. are subsistence farmers.
   b. are fishers.
   c. work on haciendas.
   d. are ranchers.

4) A llama is an
   a. animal raised for its meat.
   b. animal whose silky hair is used to make sweaters.
   c. animal related to a camel and used to carry things.
   d. animal who lives in a desert.

5) People living along the coastal areas of Colombia, Venezuela, the Guianas, and the east coast of Brazil were influenced by people from
   a. Spain.
   b. Africa.
   c. Portugal.
   d. North America.

6) The region in South America that has the fewest people is
   a. Afro-America.
   b. Euro-America.
   c. Pacific America.
   d. Indo-America.

7) People living on the pampas
   a. grew corn for a living.
   b. fished for a living.
   c. hunted wild game for a living.
   d. raised cattle for a living.

8) Most people in South America follow
   a. Judaism.
   b. Buddhism.
   c. Christianity.
   d. Hinduism.

9) Geographers expect the population of South America to
   a. decrease gradually in the next five years.
   b. double in the next 25 years.
   c. remain the same for the next 10 years.
   d. double next year.

10) South American peasants move to cities
   a. because the government told them to.
   b. because there is no land left to farm.
   c. because the cities are less crowded than rural areas.
   d. to find better jobs, schools, and health care.

Life in South America

Directions: Read each sentence. Write *T* if the statement is *true* and *F* if it is *false*.

_____ **1)** Most people in Indo-America speak their own native languages.

_____ **2)** People in Indo-America raise sheep, llamas, and alpacas.

_____ **3)** Native people are the richest people in South America.

_____ **4)** During the early settlement of Afro-America, many native people died from European diseases.

_____ **5)** Paraguay and Uruguay are part of Afro-America.

_____ **6)** Much of the population of Afro-America is descended from the Spanish.

_____ **7)** Europeans brought African slaves to work on plantations and in mines.

_____ **8)** European influence is strongest in Indo-America.

_____ **9)** Gauchos developed their own culture based on farming methods.

_____ **10)** People in larger cities of South America speak many different languages.

_____ **11)** All South Americans are Christians.

_____ **12)** South America has one of the lowest birthrates in the world.

_____ **13)** Portuguese is the official language of Brazil.

_____ **14)** São Paulo, Rio de Janeiro, and Buenos Aires are small rural areas in South America.

_____ **15)** The cities of South America are well equipped to handle many new residents.

South America's Economy and Environment

Part A Directions: Match each word with the correct definition.
Write the correct letter on the line.

_____ **1)** invest

a. business of farming with large farms and lots of chemicals and machines

_____ **2)** clear-cut

b. large company that does business in more than one country

_____ **3)** global warming

c. give or loan money in the hope of getting more money back in the future

_____ **4)** multinational corporation

d. cut down every tree in a forest

_____ **5)** agribusiness

e. rise in Earth's temperature

Part B Directions: Use each word on the left in Part A in a sentence about South America.

1) _____

_____

2) _____

_____

3) _____

_____

4) _____

_____

5) _____

_____

The British Isles Match-Up

Directions: Match the words on the left with the phrases on the right.
Write the correct letter on each line.

_____	1)	English Channel	**a.**	largest of the British Isles
_____	2)	50°–60° north latitude	**b.**	longest river in the British Isles
_____	3)	Great Britain	**c.**	mountains of Great Britain
_____	4)	Ireland	**d.**	highland region west of England
_____	5)	Republic of Ireland	**e.**	city in Wales
_____	6)	lowlands	**f.**	hilly area of Scotland and Wales
_____	7)	Shannon River	**g.**	part of North European Plain
_____	8)	Scotland	**h.**	rough land in northern Great Britain
_____	9)	England	**i.**	territory of the United Kingdom in Atlantic
_____	10)	Wales	**j.**	the "Emerald Isle"
_____	11)	Industrial Revolution	**k.**	independent nation in southern Ireland
_____	12)	Cardiff	**l.**	location of the British Isles
_____	13)	highlands	**m.**	separates the British Isles and Europe
_____	14)	Falkland Islands	**n.**	era of machines and changes in workplace
_____	15)	Pennine Chain	**o.**	birthplace of Industrial Revolution

Name _____   Date _____   Period _____

The British Isles' Climate and Physical Features

Directions: Write the correct word or words from the Word Bank to complete each sentence.

Word Bank			
gales	bogs	Ben Nevis	Pennine
Gulf Stream	heat	Scotland	marine west coast
4,406	peat	Lake District	Thames
ocean	trade	glaciers	

The highlands of the British Isles are not very high; the tallest mountain there is

1) _____, which is just 2) _____

feet tall. A mountain range that reaches from 3) _____ south into England

is the 4) _____ Chain.

5) _____ are lowland swamps where water covers plants. Over time, the

plants become 6) _____, which was used to 7) _____ homes.

8) _____ formed many lakes in the British Isles. The lovely

9) _____ of England draws many tourists. The most

famous river in England is the 10) _____, which flows through London. As

island dwellers, the people of the British Isles have a long history of going to sea to explore,

11) _____, and fish.

The British Isles have a 12) _____ climate, which

is mild due to the influence of the 13) _____. A current called the

14) _____ brings warmth from the Caribbean.

Rain and strong winds, called 15) _____, are common in western upland

areas of the British Isles.

The People of the British Isles True or False

Directions: Read each sentence. Write *T* if the statement is *true* and *F*
if it is *false*.

_____ **1)** Many different peoples invaded and settled in the British Isles throughout history.

_____ **2)** Tribes from northern Europe that invaded England were Celts and Romans.

_____ **3)** The Angles, Saxons, and Jutes were tribes that gave rise to the English people.

_____ **4)** Since 1950, most immigrants to Great Britain have come from Ireland.

_____ **5)** The Church of England is the largest Protestant group in England.

_____ **6)** Followers of the Church of Scotland are Protestants.

_____ **7)** Most people in the Republic of Ireland are Muslim.

_____ **8)** Most people in the British Isles are Roman Catholic.

_____ **9)** About half of the English language comes from the language of the Angles and Saxons.

_____ **10)** Romance languages come from the language spoken by Roman armies.

_____ **11)** Most people in the British Isles speak Celtic languages.

_____ **12)** About 100 million people live in Great Britain.

_____ **13)** The population density is highest in Scotland and Wales.

_____ **14)** Many people in Great Britain live in big cities such as London and Leeds.

_____ **15)** An urban planner studies the needs of people who live in cities.

_____ **16)** The prejudice of immigrants against the inner-city poor is a problem for Great Britain.

_____ **17)** Much of the conflict between immigrants and the poor comes from concern over jobs.

_____ **18)** Great Britain's birthrate is high.

_____ **19)** One problem with having a low birthrate is too many workers.

_____ **20)** A lower birthrate in Great Britain means that a larger percentage of the population is older.

The British Isles Multiple Choice

Directions: Circle the letter of the correct answer.

1) In a free-market economy, producers
____.
   a. are the buyers
   b. are manufacturers and farmers
   c. may do whatever they want
   d. work in factories

2) A free-market economy is based primarily
on ____.
   a. competition
   b. government control
   c. cooperation
   d. heavy industry

3) In the past, Great Britain's economy
depended on ____.
   a. insurance sales
   b. tourism
   c. heavy industry
   d. the banking industry

4) Service industries create about ____ of all
jobs in Great Britain today.
   a. one-third
   b. half
   c. two-thirds
   d. three-fourths

5) Farmers are able to produce two-thirds of
the food needed by Great Britain because
of ____.
   a. large farming regions
   b. fertile bogs
   c. large numbers of farmers
   d. new technology

6) A good example of a job in heavy
industry is a ____.
   a. farmer
   b. shipbuilder
   c. computer programmer
   d. store clerk

7) ____ is important to the economy of the
British Isles.
   a. Trade
   b. Television
   c. Coal mining
   d. Steel production

8) The most abundant natural resource of
the British Isles is ____.
   a. seafood
   b. oil
   c. coal
   d. diamonds

9) An environmental problem that troubles
the people of the British Isles is ____.
   a. too much noise
   b. air and water pollution
   c. loss of wetlands
   d. excess garbage

10) Dividing the total income in a country by
its population gives you ____.
   a. per capita income
   b. the poverty index
   c. the consumers index
   d. the ratio of imports to exports

Western Europe Paragraphs

Directions: Complete the paragraphs below. Write a word on each line.

Western Europe is made up of **1)** _____ countries. They are Germany,

the **2)** _____, Belgium, **3)** _____, Austria, **4)** _____, and

France. These countries are located in the **5)** _____ latitudes. The major bodies

of water surrounding western Europe are the **6)** _____ Sea and the

7) _____ Channel to the north, the **8)** _____ Sea to the south,

and the Bay of **9)** _____ and the **10)** _____ Ocean to the west.

Western Europe has three physical regions. The largest region is the **11)** _____. The

12) _____ form the mountainous area that covers Switzerland, parts of southeastern

France, northern Italy, southwestern Germany, Austria, and Slovenia. Between the Central Lowlands

and the Alps lie the Central **13)** _____.

The geography of western Europe has helped shape its history. Both World War I and

14) _____ were fought, at least partly, in western Europe. However, the high mountains

that surround **15)** _____ have made it hard for armies to invade this country, allowing

it to stay out of wars.

Countries that lie in the plains of the Central Lowlands, on the other hand, can easily be

16) _____ by soldiers. Thick forests and rugged mountains kept German soldiers from

attacking **17)** _____ directly during World War I. In order to reach

18) _____, the capital of France, German soldiers marched into **19)** _____.

The soldiers quickly took over nearly all of Belgium and then the industrial area of

20) _____ France.

Western Europe Match-Up

Directions: Match the words on the left with the correct description
on the right. Write the correct letter on the line.

_____ 1) Bay of Biscay

_____ 2) peaks

_____ 3) mistrals

_____ 4) French Riviera

_____ 5) the Loire

_____ 6) the Rhine

_____ 7) polders

_____ 8) Eurasia

_____ 9) passes

_____ 10) Mont Blanc

_____ 11) dikes

_____ 12) the North Sea

_____ 13) the Alps

_____ 14) the Seine

_____ 15) peninsula

a. walls built by the Dutch people to prevent floods

b. the biggest physical feature of western Europe

c. body of water that forms the western shore of France

d. the highest mountain peak in the Alps

e. area bordering the Mediterranean Sea that has mild winters and dry, hot summers

f. the largest piece of land in the world

g. river that flows through the capital of France

h. strong winds that blow cold, dry air down from the Alps

i. created when the Dutch people took back land from the sea

j. the tops of mountains

k. the longest river in France

l. Germany's most important river

m. openings in mountain ranges

n. shallow body of water that lies to the north of western Europe

o. land that is surrounded by water on three sides

Physical Features and Climate Puzzle

Directions: Write the correct word from the Word Bank to complete the sentences.

Word Bank				
peninsula	Alps	mistrals	Hamburg	polders
Eurasia	Mont Blanc	marine	Netherlands	dikes

1) The _____ are the biggest physical feature in western Europe.

2) Half of the _____ is made up of polder land.

3) _____ are walls built to prevent floods.

4) Western Europe is described by some as a large _____.

5) _____ stands 15,771 feet tall.

6) The Dutch people use huge electric pumps to keep seawater from returning to the

_____.

7) Western Europe is located on the western part of _____.

8) The main climate of western Europe is a _____ west coast climate.

9) The _____ cause temperatures in southern France to drop quickly.

10) _____ is a German harbor located where the Elbe meets the North Sea.

Use five of the words from the sentences to fill in the words in the puzzle. The letters in the box spell the name of one of western Europe's most important rivers.

11) ___ ___ ___ ___ | ___ | ___ ___ ___

12)   ___ ___ ___ | ___ | ___   ___ ___ ___ ___

13)   ___ ___ ___ | ___ | ___ ___ ___ ___

14)   ___ ___ | ___ | ___ ___ ___ ___ ___ ___

15)   ___ | ___ | ___ ___ ___ ___ ___ ___

All About the People

Directions: Choose the word from the Word Bank that best completes each
sentence. Write your answer on the line.

Word Bank				
aging	culture	dialect	population	Germanic
Latin	Munich	religious	soccer	Switzerland

1) _____ is a popular sport in western Europe.

2) Each country in western Europe has its own _____, yet
the countries also have much in common.

3) German and Dutch are both _____ languages.

4) Most people in Switzerland speak a German _____.

5) _____ was the language of the ancient Romans.

6) Romansh is one of the official languages of _____.

7) Western Europe has one of the highest _____ densities
in the world.

8) Many European countries fought in a _____ war from
1618 to 1648.

9) The cities of Hamburg, Berlin, and _____ have more
than a million people each.

10) Western Europe has an _____ population.

Economy and Environment Puzzle

Directions: Use the clues below to complete the puzzle.

Down

1) _____ pollution is one of western Europe's environmental challenges.
3) Western European farmers grow many grains, especially _____.
5) The _____ River is so polluted that many people do not want to eat its fish.
6) The Netherlands exports _____ around the world.
7) One country selling its goods to another country is an example of _____ trade.
8) To create closer ties with one another, several western European countries agreed to get rid of _____.
12) _____ from France are world famous.

Across

2) One of France's few natural resources is _____.
4) Fast-flowing rivers provide the source for _____.
9) French _____ are world famous.
10) _____, which are used to make wine, are an important crop in western Europe.
11) France produces more _____ than any other country in the world.
13) Switzerland is famous for its _____.
14) In France, _____ are used to produce power.
15) The Euro will replace the _____ that each country has now.

Describing Southern Europe

Part A Directions: Complete the table with words from the Word Bank. List the bodies of water under the name of the peninsula they surround. Some may be used two times.

Word Bank

Aegean Sea	Bay of Biscay	Mediterranean Sea
Atlantic Ocean	Adriatic Sea	Strait of Gibraltar
Ionian Sea	Tyrrhenian Sea	Ligurian Sea

Iberian Peninsula   **Italian Peninsula**   **Balkan Peninsula**

_____   _____   _____

_____   _____   _____

_____   _____

_____   _____

Part B Directions: Write each phrase from the Word Bank under the nation it describes. Some phrases may be used more than one time.

Word Bank

mostly dry highland	Costa del Sol	largest in area of the four nations
three-fourths mountains	mostly meseta	the Algarve
drained swamps for farmland		

Spain   **Portugal**

_____   _____

_____   _____

_____

Italy   **Greece**

_____   _____

_____   _____

Mountains, Islands, Water

Directions: Complete the paragraphs. Write the correct words from
the Word Bank to complete the sentences.

Word Bank				
Crete	Cantabrians	Apennine	Sardinia	Po
Sicily	Achelous	Maggiore	Alps	Corfu
Balearic	Como	Garda	Guadalquivir	Tiber
Pyrenees	Rhodes	Canary	Ebro	Pindus

Spain has two mountain ranges in the north: **1)** _____ and

2) _____. Its most important rivers are the **3)** _____

and the **4)** _____. Important islands off the coast of Spain are the

5) _____ Islands and the **6)** _____ Islands.

The **7)** _____ Mountains border northern Italy.

The **8)** _____ Mountains form the backbone of Italy. The

9) _____ is the only navigable river in Italy; other important rivers there

are the **10)** _____, Arno, Dora, and Taro. Famous Italian lakes are Lake

11) _____, Lake **12)** _____, and Lake

13) _____. Two large islands off Italy's coast are **14)** _____

and **15)** _____.

Greece's biggest mountain range is the **16)** _____ Mountains.

17) _____, **18)** _____, and **19)** _____

are the largest of Greece's many islands. The **20)** _____ is the longest river in

Greece.

The People of Southern Europe

Directions: Read each sentence. Write *T* if the statement is *true* and *F* if it is *false*.

_____ **1)** The countries of southern Europe all have similar cultural backgrounds.

_____ **2)** The Portuguese were influenced by Iberians, Celts, Romans, and Moors.

_____ **3)** Italians call their country Hellas and themselves Hellenes.

_____ **4)** The Turks ruled Greece for many years.

_____ **5)** Families made up of parents, children, grandparents, aunts, uncles, cousins, and others are traditional families.

_____ **6)** Tradition, history, and religion are important to southern Europeans.

_____ **7)** Most people in Greece, Italy, and Spain are Roman Catholic.

_____ **8)** Vatican City in Rome, Italy, is considered an independent nation.

_____ **9)** The Greek Orthodox Church was once part of the Roman Catholic Church.

_____ **10)** Portuguese, Spanish, and Greek are Romance languages.

_____ **11)** All the people of Italy speak only Italian.

_____ **12)** Madrid and Barcelona are major cities in Spain.

_____ **13)** Most southern Europeans live in rural areas.

_____ **14)** Italy and Spain are the most urban of the southern European nations.

_____ **15)** Athens is the capital city of Portugal.

_____ **16)** The Basques are a people with great loyalty to Spain.

_____ **17)** Regionalism is loyalty more to one part of a country than to the whole country.

_____ **18)** Italy became a united nation in 1871.

_____ **19)** Galileo determined that objects of varying sizes all fall at the same speed.

_____ **20)** Galileo was the first to believe that Earth revolves around the Sun.

Southern Europe Match-Up

Directions: Match the words on the left with the correct description
on the right. Write the correct letter on the line.

_____ 1) European Union

_____ 2) inflation

_____ 3) marble

_____ 4) agriculture

_____ 5) industry

_____ 6) bauxite

_____ 7) cork

_____ 8) fruit

_____ 9) textiles

_____ 10) tourism

_____ 11) flooding

_____ 12) Venice

_____ 13) chemicals

_____ 14) soil erosion

_____ 15) goats

a. topsoil washed or blown away

b. oldest, most important industry in Italy

c. built on supports sunk into the sea

d. period of rising prices

e. a problem with water in Italy

f. organization of nations to strengthen economy

g. basis for strong economy of Italy

h. mineral that Italy produces in huge amounts

i. Spain's biggest agricultural export

j. one reason for soil erosion

k. used by industry and agriculture; pollute water

l. principal export of Portugal

m. important mineral of Greece

n. pre-World War II basis for economy

o. industry important to all of southern Europe

Northern Europe

Directions: Read each sentence. Write *T* if the statement is *true* or *F* if it is *false*.

_____ **1)** Northern Europe lies entirely within the Arctic Circle.

_____ **2)** Norway and Sweden share a peninsula.

_____ **3)** The Baltic Sea lies between Denmark and Finland.

_____ **4)** The climate in northern Europe is very warm.

_____ **5)** People in northern Europe have long had close ties to the sea.

_____ **6)** The Vikings sailed from Scandinavia to many other parts of the world.

_____ **7)** The Vikings sailed to North America before Columbus did.

_____ **8)** Russia is part of northern Europe.

_____ **9)** Iceland was formed by earthquakes.

_____ **10)** The Icelandic people build their houses out of concrete because there is a shortage of trees.

_____ **11)** Denmark is one of the flattest countries in the world.

_____ **12)** Most of the people in Norway live along the coast.

_____ **13)** The biggest cities in Sweden are located in the north.

_____ **14)** Finland lies south of Sweden.

_____ **15)** Glaciers formed Finland's plain.

All About Northern Europe

Directions: Complete the paragraphs below. Write a word on each line.

There are four main physical features in northern Europe. Long, deep, narrow ocean

inlets, known as **1)** _____, are the best known feature of Iceland and Norway.

2) _____ are another physical feature. They are still being formed by

3) _____. **4)** _____ are a third important feature.

Only the **5)** _____ in western Europe are higher than Norway's mountains.

6) _____ are common in Iceland; they provide a source of **7)** _____

energy for heating homes.

Northern Europe has thousands of **8)** _____, which were left behind when

9) _____ melted. **10)** Lake _____ in Sweden is northern Europe's largest

lake.

The climate of northern Europe is varied. The mountain areas have **11)** _____

climates. However, the coastal areas are warmed by the **12)** _____ and have a

more **13)** _____ climate. Because the countries of northern Europe lie so far

14) _____, they have great differences between daylight and night. On the

15) _____, the sun never sets. During winter, there are days when the people

never see the sun.

Understanding the People of Northern Europe

Directions: Write the correct word from the Word Bank to complete each sentence. Not all words from the Word Bank are used.

Word Bank				
Sami	alike	Swedish	English	different
elevation	welfare	birthrate	homogenous	Copenhagen
Stockholm	nomads	Lutheran	declining	refugees

1) The cultures of Scandinavia are _____.

2) Because most Scandinavians are descended from Germanic tribes, the population

   of northern Europe is _____.

3) _____ from the former Yugoslavia, Turkey, Vietnam, and the
   Middle East live in the big cities of Scandinavia.

4) The _____ are the largest minority group in Norway, Sweden,
   and Finland.

5) _____ are people who move from place to place.

6) The _____ Church is the official church of northern Europe.

7) _____ is Finland's second official language.

8) _____ is Scandinavia's biggest city.

9) One reason for northern Europe's slow population growth is its low

   _____.

10) Scandinavian workers pay high taxes to support northern Europe's

   _____ system.

The Economy and Environment of Northern Europe

Directions: Circle the letter of the correct answer.

1) An economic system in which the government controls many of the biggest industries is called ____.
   a. imperialism
   b. free enterprise
   c. socialism
   d. capitalism

2) Norway's most important resource is ____.
   a. oil
   b. iron
   c. copper
   d. zinc

3) The mining of minerals in northern Europe has not been developed fully because ____.
   a. of a lack of workers
   b. the minerals are hard to get to
   c. it is not profitable
   d. there is no demand

4) Both Finland and Sweden use their forests ____.
   a. for hydroelectric power
   b. to test nuclear weapons
   c. in paper and pulp-making industries
   d. as a highway to the sawmills

5) More than half of all Scandinavian workers work in ____.
   a. service industries
   b. forestry
   c. the paper industry
   d. mining

6) The Scandinavian country that manufactures the most products is ____.
   a. Norway
   b. Finland
   c. Iceland
   d. Sweden

7) Norway is the world's second largest exporter of ____.
   a. forest products
   b. metal products
   c. plastics
   d. electronic goods

8) Shipping is a key industry in northern Europe because of ____.
   a. its extensive supply of wood
   b. the high demand for fish
   c. its closeness to the sea
   d. the long days in summer

9) Aquaculture, an important industry in Norway, is another name for ____.
   a. hydroelectric power
   b. recreational water sports
   c. tourism in the coastal areas
   d. fish farming

10) Northern Europe's rate for recycling aluminum, glass, and paper is one of the highest in the world because ____.
   a. Scandinavians appreciate nature
   b. they receive money for recycling these products
   c. there is a shortage of these materials
   d. it is cheaper to recycle than to pay for garbage collection services

Eastern Europe and the Balkan Countries

Directions: Complete the paragraphs. Write the word(s) to complete each sentence.

    Eastern Europe and the Balkan countries are located in the **1)** _____

latitudes. Eastern Europe includes the countries of Poland, the Czech Republic, Slovakia,

and **2)** _____. Poland is the only eastern European country that is not landlocked

because the **3)** _____ borders it on the north. The **4)** _____ countries

include Romania, Bulgaria, Albania, and the former Yugoslavia. The combined population of all the

countries in this area is about **5)** _____ million.

    Eastern Europe and the Balkans have four regions. They are the **6)** _____

_____, which stretches across western and eastern Europe;

a region of mountains and rugged hills that cover **7)** _____ and parts of the

Czech Republic and Romania; another **8)** _____, which lies between the

9) _____ Mountains and the Balkan Peninsula; and the Balkan

10) _____ itself.

    The history of this region has been greatly influenced by its geography.

11) _____ has been invaded many times by its neighbors because it is one large, flat

area. Because of these invasions, its borders have changed often. The Balkan countries were

controlled by **12)** _____ for over 400 years. This mountainous area was hard to

govern because people were isolated from one another. This isolation led to the development of

different **13)** _____. The differences between groups made them distrust each other,

which led to **14)** _____. The old Turkish Empire was **15)** _____ by the

winners of World War I—the region was broken up into smaller political areas.

Land, Water, and Climate Puzzle

Directions: Write the correct word from the Word Bank to complete each sentence.

Word Bank				
Alps	beets	Danube	Lake Balaton	lakes
mountains	narrows	plains	Rhodope	

1) Farmers grow _____, grains, and tobacco on the plains of eastern Europe.

2) The _____ is the most important river of eastern Europe and the Balkans.

3) _____ are the second of eastern Europe's main physical features.

4) The Dinaric _____ run along the Adriatic Coast.

5) Northern Poland has over 9,000 _____.

6) _____ is located in Hungary.

7) The _____ Mountains are the highest mountains in the Balkan Peninsula.

8) Eastern Europe's main physical feature is its _____.

9) The Iron Gate is a _____ on the Danube River.

Use the words from the sentences to fill in the words in the puzzle. The letters in the box spell the Turkish word for mountain.

10) ___ A ___ ___ |___| E

11) ___|___|___ ___ S

12) ___|___| P ___

13) L ___|___|___ B ___ ___ ___ ___ ___ ___

14) P ___|___|___ N ___

15) ___|___ R ___ ___ ___ S

Vocabulary Match-Up

Directions: Match the words on the left with the correct description on the right. Write the correct letter on the line.

_____ **1)** cultural crossroad

a. a group of people who have a common language, culture, and set of values

_____ **2)** Slavic

b. followers of Islam

_____ **3)** ethnic group

c. not having enough of something

_____ **4)** Cyrillic alphabet

d. things people buy for themselves and for their homes

_____ **5)** concentration camp

e. having to do with people from central Asia who settled in eastern Europe

_____ **6)** Holocaust

f. a place where different cultures come into contact with one another

_____ **7)** Muslims

g. a large prison death camp

_____ **8)** Islam

h. an alphabet that began in about A.D. 900 and was used to translate the Bible into Slavic languages

_____ **9)** consumer goods

i. the attempt by Germany's Nazi Party to kill all the Jews in Europe during World War II

_____ **10)** shortage

j. religion brought to the Balkans by the Turks

Matching Economic and Environmental Terms

Directions: Write the word(s) from the Word Bank that fit(s) each clue.

Word Bank			
communism	lignite	pitchblende	water pollution
Romania	developing country	heavy industry	sulfur
	Russia	Hungary	

1) most of eastern Europe depends on this country for minerals and energy resources

   _____

2) soft, brown coal found in several eastern European and Balkan countries

   _____

3) produces goods that are used to produce other goods

   _____

4) major environmental problem for eastern Europe and the Balkans

   _____

5) a system where government owns most of the property and produces most of the goods

   _____

6) with Poland and the Czech Republic, one of the most industrialized countries in this area

   _____

7) only country in eastern Europe that had oil and natural gas

   _____

8) by-product of lignite that contributes to acid rain

   _____

9) a place where people are often poor and many of them are farmers

   _____

10) ore containing radium

   _____

Facts About Russia and the Independent Republics

Directions: Circle the word(s) in parentheses that best complete(s) each sentence.

1) Russia has (nine, eleven) time zones.

2) The United States is (bigger, smaller) than Russia.

3) The (Bering Sea, Baltic Sea) separates Russia from Alaska.

4) China and Iran are (west, south) of Russia.

5) Besides Russia, there are (fourteen, twelve) other independent republics.

6) Russia and the other independent republics were formerly part of (the Soviet Union, China).

7) Each of the independent republics has its own (dictator, constitution).

8) All of the republics, except for Estonia, Latvia, and (Belarus, Lithuania), are members of the Commonwealth of Independent States.

9) The largest cities of Russia are located in (Central Asia, the Russian plain).

10) (The Russian plain, Siberia) is the largest region.

11) Much of central Asia is a (flat lowland with many rivers, desertlike area).

12) In the 1200s, the (Mongols, Vikings) invaded the Russian plains.

13) The (Baltic States, Ural Mountains) divide Russia.

14) The (western, eastern) part of Russia is largely uninhabited.

15) Russia's (climate, population) has greatly influenced its history.

Features of Russia and the Independent Republics

Directions: Write the word(s) from the Word Bank that best complete(s) each sentence.

Word Bank				
polar	Black Sea	steppe	Caspian Sea	tundra
plains	hydroelectric	Lake Baykal	driest	subarctic

1) The most common physical feature of the region are _____.

2) Most of the northern part of Russia is _____.

3) The Caucasus Mountains lie between the Caspian Sea and the _____.

4) The _____ forms part of Russia's southern border.

5) Many of Russia's rivers are a source of _____ power.

6) _____ contains 80 percent of Russia's freshwater supply.

7) The southern Ukraine has a _____ climate.

8) A _____ climate has long, cold winters and short, warm summers.

9) The taiga has a _____ climate.

10) The republics of central Asia have the _____ climate of the region.

Land and Climate

Directions: Circle the letter of the correct answer.

1) The tundra is _____.
   a. the world's largest forest
   b. a flat, treeless plain
   c. an area of rich, fertile soil
   d. an area at the mouth of a river

2) Both the tundra and the taiga _____.
   a. are sparsely populated
   b. are home to many trees
   c. have many active volcanoes
   d. border the Pacific Ocean

3) The Caucasus Mountains are the primary feature of _____.
   a. Belarus and Latvia
   b. Moldova and Tajikistan
   c. Estonia and Uzbekistan
   d. Georgia, Armenia, and Azerbaijan

4) The Kamchatka Peninsula is in _____.
   a. eastern Siberia
   b. St. Petersburg
   c. Kiev
   d. central Asia

5) The Volga River flows into the _____.
   a. Pacific Ocean
   b. Black Sea
   c. Caspian Sea
   d. Arctic Ocean

6) The Angara, Lena, Ob, and Yenisey Rivers flow into _____.
   a. the Black Sea
   b. the Arctic Ocean
   c. the Pacific Ocean
   d. Lake Baykal

7) Russian rivers are important because _____.
   a. there is no other source of freshwater
   b. the people enjoy boating
   c. there are few good roads and railroads
   d. fishing is an important part of the Russian economy

8) Russia and the other republics have many different climates because they _____.
   a. are surrounded by water
   b. are close to the Arctic Circle
   c. cover such a large area
   d. are far away from the equator

9) The climate of European Russia is similar to the climate of _____.
   a. Ireland
   b. Central America
   c. the southern part of the United States
   d. the midwestern part of the United States

10) The area that receives the least amount of rainfall is _____.
   a. southern Ukraine
   b. northern Russia
   c. the republics of central Asia
   d. European Russia

Cultures of Russia and the Independent Republics

Directions: Read each sentence. Write *T* if the statement is *true* or *F* if
it is *false*.

_____   **1)**   The Russians are the largest ethnic group in this region.

_____   **2)**   Many people of the republics in central Asia are descendants of the Celts.

_____   **3)**   Russian and other Slavic languages use the Cyrillic alphabet.

_____   **4)**   When the Communists took control of Russia, many people worshiped at home.

_____   **5)**   Communist rule in Russia came to an end in 2000.

_____   **6)**   The main religion of the region is Russian Orthodox.

_____   **7)**   Hinduism is the second largest religion in Russia.

_____   **8)**   Moscow is the capital of Ukraine.

_____   **9)**   St. Petersburg is Russia's biggest seaport on the Baltic Sea.

_____   **10)**   The Kremlin is the political center of the CIS.

_____   **11)**   Moscow is well-known for its museums and cultural activities.

_____   **12)**   The people of Chechnya want to form an independent country.

_____   **13)**   Religious and ethnic differences have caused war in Armenia, Georgia, and Azerbaijan.

_____   **14)**   In March 2000, the Russian people elected Boris Yeltsin to be their president.

_____   **15)**   The Russian government provides many services for its citizens.

Economy and Environment

Directions: Match the words on the left with the correct description on the right.
Write the correct letter on the line.

_____ **1)** collective farm

a. environmental hazard produced by atomic power plants

_____ **2)** command economy

b. selling state farmland to private owners

_____ **3)** market economy

c. economy in which there are privately owned businesses

_____ **4)** privatization

d. large, state-owned property worked by the people

_____ **5)** nuclear waste

e. economy in which the government makes the key economic decisions

Use each word in the list above in a sentence about Russia or the independent republics.

6) _____

_____

7) _____

_____

8) _____

_____

9) _____

_____

10) _____

_____

West Africa

Directions: Complete the paragraphs. Write the correct word(s) from
the Word Bank to complete each sentence.

Word Bank				
2.3 million	mangrove	equator	deltas	timber
coastal plain	sixteen	Guinea	fuel	desertification
shore	tsetse	black	savanna	Sahara

West Africa covers **1)** _____ square miles and lies between

the **2)** _____ and 20° north latitude. It has **3)** _____

countries. The Atlantic Ocean and the Gulf of **4)** _____ border

many of these countries.

It has four physical regions. The first region includes two **5)** _____

of the Niger River. The inland delta is a huge wetland with lots of tropical

6) _____ trees. The second region is a wide **7)** _____

that was once covered with tropical rain forests. The trees were cut down to be used for

8) _____ and exported as **9)** _____. The

10) _____ is good for farming. However, the **11)** _____

fly and the **12)** _____ fly live there and cause diseases. The Sahel

is on the **13)** "_____" or edge of the **14)** _____.

It is becoming a desert itself through the process of **15)** _____.

What It's Like in West Africa

Directions: Write the answers to these questions using complete sentences.

1) Why are harbors in West Africa hard for ships to use?

_____

2) What is the land like in most of West Africa?

_____

3) How did the Sierra Leone mountain range get its name?

_____

_____

4) What are escarpments and what do they do?

_____

_____

5) Why is the Niger River important to West Africa?

_____

_____

6) What is the climate of West Africa like?

_____

7) Which region is rainy, and how much rain does it get?

_____

8) How does the climate change as you go north?

_____

9) What kind of climate does the Sahel region have?

_____

10) What is the harmattan and what does it do?

_____

The West Africans True or False

Directions: Read each sentence. Write *T* if the statement is *true* or *F* if it is *false*.

_____ **1)** West Africa has hundreds of different ethnic groups.

_____ **2)** West African cultivators herd animals and are sometimes nomads.

_____ **3)** The Fulani and Tuareg peoples are pastoralists.

_____ **4)** Only French, English, and Portuguese are spoken in West Africa.

_____ **5)** Most Christian West Africans live along the coast, and most Muslim West Africans live in the north.

_____ **6)** Many rural West Africans believe things in nature contain spirits.

_____ **7)** Most West Africans live in shantytowns.

_____ **8)** Subsistence farmers grow what they need to eat and not much more.

_____ **9)** Many Muslims have large families because men can have up to four wives.

_____ **10)** People in shantytowns live well.

_____ **11)** West African countries have population problems because of a low birthrate.

_____ **12)** The growth rate of many West African countries is 2 percent to 4 percent a year.

_____ **13)** Low life expectancy is West Africa's biggest problem.

_____ **14)** Four of the five poorest countries in the world are in West Africa.

_____ **15)** Ibrahima was a West African prince who spent 42 years in slavery in the United States.

_____ **16)** Many West Africans are hungry because there is too little food.

_____ **17)** Many of West Africa's problems were caused by wars with European nations.

_____ **18)** Rulers of West African countries have often been dishonest.

_____ **19)** A coup is a sudden overthrow of a government.

_____ **20)** Most West African nations have been independent since the 1950s and 1960s.

West Africa Match-Up

Directions: Match the words on the left with the correct description
on the right. Write the correct letter on the line.

_____ 1) subsistence farmers   **a.** cacao, coffee, peanuts, cotton

_____ 2) staple crops   **b.** cassavas, yams, corn, millet, sorghum

_____ 3) intercropping   **c.** things used to make finished products

_____ 4) shifting agriculture   **d.** deforestation, erosion, desertification

_____ 5) cash crops   **e.** more imports than exports

_____ 6) Côte d'Ivoire   **f.** cut down faster than they are replaced

_____ 7) raw materials   **g.** world's largest producer of cacao

_____ 8) trade imbalance   **h.** planting different crops together in one field

_____ 9) rain forests   **i.** farmers move to new land every few years

_____ 10) environmental problems   **j.** raise crops for their families to eat

_____ 11) root crops   **k.** loss of forests in an area

_____ 12) erosion   **l.** land that can grow crops

_____ 13) fertile   **m.** crops such as cassavas and yams

_____ 14) deforestation   **n.** products sold by one country to another country

_____ 15) exports   **o.** soil washed away by water or blown away by wind

Southern Africa Facts

Directions: Circle the letter of the correct answer.

1) Southern Africa stretches from about
   a. 10° north latitude to about 10° south latitude.
   b. 10° to about 35° south latitude.
   c. 10° to about 35° north latitude.
   d. 20° to about 55° south latitude.

2) Angola, Zambia, Malawi, and Mozambique are
   a. located near southern Africa's tip.
   b. covered by a desert.
   c. all landlocked countries.
   d. located in the northern part of southern Africa.

3) Madagascar, the Seychelles, the Comoros, and Mauritius are
   a. island nations of southern Africa.
   b. located in the Atlantic Ocean.
   c. on the west side of southern Africa.
   d. the southernmost countries in southern Africa.

4) The Portuguese found the southern tip of Africa as they were
   a. helping the Dutch build a settlement.
   b. searching for gold.
   c. exploring land routes to Asia.
   d. looking for a sea route to Asia.

5) The southern tip of Africa is called
   a. the Cape of Good News.
   b. the Cape of Good Hope.
   c. Johannesburg.
   d. Kalahari.

6) Gold was found on a farm in South Africa in
   a. the 1400s.
   b. 1652.
   c. 1950.
   d. 1886.

7) The Little Karroo plateau, the Great Karroo plateau, and the Drakensburg Mountains make up the
   a. veld.
   b. low-lying plain.
   c. highland region.
   d. large desert region.

8) Malawi is called the "Switzerland of Africa" because
   a. it lies in the Alps.
   b. its people speak German, French, and Italian.
   c. of its beautiful mountain scenery.
   d. it is landlocked.

9) The veld
   a. is covered with forests.
   b. often floods during heavy rains.
   c. covers much of Namibia.
   d. has rich soil for growing grain.

10) Heavy rains often cause flooding in the coastal plain of
   a. Lesotho.
   b. Mozambique.
   c. Swaziland.
   d. Zimbabwe.

Physical Features of Southern Africa

Directions: Match each term on the left with the correct description
on the right. Write the correct letter on each line.

_____ 1) Lake Kariba

  a. weather factor; these usually blow from the
     same direction

_____ 2) pans

  b. dams on the Zambezi River provide this

_____ 3) Namib

  c. land formation often seen in southern Africa

_____ 4) hydroelectric power

  d. climate with hot, humid summers and
     mild winters

_____ 5) prevailing winds

  e. climate type of the southernmost tip of Africa

_____ 6) plateau

  f. dry area where few plants grow

_____ 7) Mediterranean

  g. salt lakes

_____ 8) Indian Ocean

  h. ninth largest desert in the world

_____ 9) Kalahari

  i. human-made body of water

_____ 10) subtropical

  j. body of water into which the Zambezi
     River empties

Southern Africa Culture Puzzle

Directions: Write the correct word(s) from the Word Bank to complete the sentences.

		Word Bank		
Niger	San	Netherlands	civil unrest	apartheid
animism	Mozambique	Khoisan	Islam	Dutch Reformed

1) Many people in _____ are Roman Catholic Christians.

2) Many Protestant Christians of Namibia and the Republic of South Africa belong

   to the _____ Church.

3) Many black Africans speak one of the _____, or Bantu, languages.

4) Many people in the northern coastal areas of Mozambique practice _____.

5) The San people speak _____.

6) Some people in southern Africa practice traditional religions like _____.

7) The ancestors of Afrikaners came from the _____.

8) _____ is a system of "apartness" that once existed in the Republic of South Africa.

9) _____ occurred when people rebelled because they were unhappy with the
   conditions in the Republic of South Africa.

10) The _____, or "Bushmen," were the earliest settlers of the Republic of South Africa.

Use the words from the sentences to complete the puzzle. The letters in the box name the group of
people in the Republic of South Africa whose ancestors came from the Netherlands.

11) __ __ __ | __ __ __ __ __ __ __ __ __
12) __ __ __ __ __ | __ __ __ __ __ __ __
13) __ __ __ __ __ | __ __ __ __ __
14) | __ __ __ __ __
15) | __ __ __ __ __ __
16) | __ __ __ __ __ __
17) | __ __ __ __ __ __ __ __
18) __ __ __ __ __ __ | __ __ __
19) __ __ __ __ __ __ __ | __ __ __
20) | __ __ __

Southern Africa's Economy and Environment

Directions: Read each sentence. Write *T* if the statement is *true* or *F* if it is *false.*

_____ 1) Most southern African people are subsistence farmers.

_____ 2) Sorghum is the main crop in Mozambique.

_____ 3) Corn is the main crop in Lesotho and Zimbabwe.

_____ 4) Service industries are the second largest employer in the Republic of South Africa.

_____ 5) Many people in southern African countries work two jobs.

_____ 6) Sugarcane is grown on plantations in Swaziland.

_____ 7) The climate of Botswana and Namibia is good for farming.

_____ 8) In Botswana and Namibia, cows are both a source of food and transportation.

_____ 9) Minerals are the chief exports of several countries in southern Africa.

_____ 10) Many people in southern African work in the mines because mining is an easy job.

_____ 11) The Republic of South Africa has the largest coal deposits in Africa.

_____ 12) Angola exports 60 percent of its copper to the United States.

_____ 13) The landscape and wildlife of southern Africa are important natural resources.

_____ 14) Angola is the richest and most industrial country in southern Africa.

_____ 15) Southern Africa's biggest problem is that it has too many people and too little farmland.

Paragraph Completion

Directions: Complete the paragraphs. Write a word on each line.

Central and East Africa are located in a wide belt north and south of the

1) _____. They are bordered by the Indian Ocean on the east and the

2) _____ Ocean on the west. The **3)** _____

is located to the north, and Southern Africa is located to the south. Central Africa is made

up of **4)** _____ countries. East Africa has **5)** _____

countries. The countries of Djibouti, Eritrea, Ethiopia, and Somalia form a horn-shaped

area called the **6)** _____.

People have lived in Africa for millions of years. Europeans settled in the

7) _____ areas where the climate is not too hot and the land is good for

8) _____. The **9)** _____ government

built a railroad to encourage settlement by Europeans. The city of **10)** _____

grew along this rail line.

Geography has kept people from settling in certain parts of Central and East Africa.

The **11)** _____ fly kept people out of the Serengeti Plain. Thick tropical

rain forests made travel through the **12)** _____ difficult, so people chose

to live in the nearby grasslands.

The location of East Africa makes it important for **13)** _____ reasons.

14) _____ from the Middle East is shipped through the

15) _____ and the Gulf of Aden. Because of this, the United States wants

to keep this area free of conflict.

Land and Climate Puzzler

Directions: Complete each statement by writing the missing letters. Then use the letters in parentheses to spell the name of one of Africa's largest lakes.

1) (___) ___ ___ ___ ___ ___ ___ ___ forests cover the Ruwenzori Mountains of Uganda.

2) Lake ___ ___ ___ ___ ___ ___ ___ (___) is Africa's largest lake.

3) Flamingos like Lake (___) ___ ___ ___ ___ ___ in Kenya.

4) The ___ ___ ___ (___) ___ is the most important river in Central Africa.

5) Because heat evaporates lake water, many of Africa's lakes are too ___ (___) ___ ___ ___ for most animals.

6) The (___) ___ ___ ___ is the longest river in the world.

7) A drought is a long ___ ___ (___) period.

8) Lake ___ ___ ___ ___ ___ (___) is one of Africa's largest lakes.

9) (___) ___ ___ ___ ___ ___ ___ ___ ___ ___ is Africa's highest mountain.

10) The Blue Nile is called the ___ ___ ___ (___) ___ in Ethiopia.

One of Africa's largest lakes is ___ ___ ___ ___ ___ ___ ___ ___ ___ ___.

Knowing the People of Central and East Africa

Directions: Write the correct word(s) from the Word Bank to complete each sentence. Some words will not be used.

Word Bank				
Bantu	Cushite	Ge'ez	Islam	mosque
Niger-Congo	Nilotic	starvation	Swahili	Mexico City
plate tectonics	corn	temples		

1) _____ is the official language of Kenya and Tanzania.

2) Some cities in Central and East Africa have Hindu _____.

3) The _____ people are an African cultural group that mostly herds animals for a living.

4) People in the Horn of Africa speak _____ languages.

5) Muslim traders brought _____ to East Africa.

6) Millions of people in East Africa face _____.

7) _____ is an old language used only in religious services.

8) A _____ is an Islamic house of worship.

9) The _____ are an African cultural group that mostly farms for a living.

10) Most people in Central Africa and the southern part of East Africa speak one

of the _____ languages.

Economy and Environment Crossword Puzzle

Directions: Read each clue. Choose a word from the Word Bank to complete the puzzle.

Across

3) The Atlantic coast of Cameroon, Gabon, and the Congo has ____.
5) A natural resource found in Gabon is ____.
7) One of Central and East Africa's most common freshwater fish is ____.
8) The growing of flowers, fruits, and vegetables for sale is called ____.
9) Large deposits of ____ are found in Congo.
11) ____ animals are ones that may become extinct.
13) The ____ Game Reserve is larger than the whole country of Switzerland.

Down

1) Congo produces over 60 percent of the world's ____.
2) ____ in the national parks is common.
4) A ____ is an African hunting trip.
5) A ____ is a person who makes all the laws for a country and rules by force.
6) Many tourists come to the ____ to see wildlife.
7) ____ is important to the economy of Central and East Africa.
10) Lack of ____ is a problem for many farmers.
12) ____ is found in both Kenya and Tanzania.

Word Bank

cobalt

diamonds

dictator

endangered

gold

horticulture

iron

oil

poaching

roads

safari

Selous

Serengeti

tilapia

tourism

Facts About North Africa and the Middle East

Directions: Circle the word(s) in parentheses that best complete(s) each sentence.

1) The Mediterranean Sea borders North Africa to the (north, south).

2) The (Plateau of Anatolia, Sahara) is on North Africa's southern border.

3) Morocco, Algeria, and Tunisia are (island nations, the Maghreb nations).

4) The Middle East is part of (Asia, Europe).

5) There are (twelve, fifteen) Middle Eastern countries.

6) (Qatar, Cyprus) is an island nation in the Mediterranean Sea.

7) North Africa and the Middle East have (four, six) subregions.

8) A narrow coastal plain in Morocco and (Algeria, Bahrain) has the most fertile soil.

9) The (Levant, Plateau of Anatolia) is a mountainous region that has many earthquakes.

10) The (Jordan River, Nile) gives Egypt fertile farmland.

11) The (Nile River Basin, Fertile Crescent) lies between the Tigris and Euphrates Rivers and the Jordan River.

12) The (Rub'al Khali, Sahara) is a large desert on the interior plateau of the Arabian Peninsula.

13) The (Egyptians, Phoenicians) developed their own culture because the deserts on either side of the Nile separated them from their neighbors.

14) The Phoenicians were traders who lived in present-day (Tunisia, Lebanon).

15) As a result of many people fighting over this area near the Mediterranean Sea, it has (a diverse culture, one culture).

Physical Features of North Africa and the Middle East

Directions: Write the correct word(s) from the Word Bank to complete each sentence.

Word Bank

desert	Red Sea	Nile	silt	sirocco
Atlas Mountains	Persian Gulf	Pontic Mountains	Aswan Dam	oasis

---

1) The main physical feature of this region is _____.

2) The _____ are in northern Turkey.

3) The _____ stretch across Morocco, Algeria, and Tunisia.

4) The flooding of the northern Great Rift Valley formed the _____.

5) A(n) _____ is a desert area with enough freshwater to grow crops or sustain life.

6) The _____ forms a 100-mile-long delta where it meets the sea.

7) The Tigris and Euphrates Rivers empty into the _____.

8) The fertile soil and small rocky pieces left behind by floodwater

is called _____.

9) Lake Nasser was created by the _____.

10) A _____ is a hot, dusty summer wind that sweeps northward from the Sahara.

North Africa and the Middle East Culture Match-Up

Directions: Match the terms on the left with the correct description
on the right. Write the correct letter on the line.

_____ 1) scholar

_____ 2) Al-Idrisi

_____ 3) Berbers

_____ 4) epic

_____ 5) Persia

_____ 6) monotheism

_____ 7) hajj

_____ 8) Kurdish

_____ 9) Cairo

_____ 10) Palestinian Liberation
Organization

a. long poem about ancient heroes

b. pilgrimage to Mecca that is a religious duty of all
Muslims, if they can afford it

c. expert in at least one subject

d. language spoken by the Kurds

e. ancestors of many North Africans

f. largest city in Egypt

g. present-day Iran

h. early Arabian geographer and mapmaker

i. organization of Arabs in Palestine who want their
own homeland

j. belief in only one god

North Africa and the Middle East Crossword Puzzle

Directions: Read each clue. Choose a word from the Word Bank to complete the puzzle.

Across
1) Muslim place of worship
3) ninth month of the Muslim calendar
5) European language spoken by many people in North Africa
7) country that invaded Kuwait and took over its oil fields
8) language closely tied to Islam
9) oldest of the three major religions of the Middle East
10) large city in Iran

Down
2) situation in which a person trained for one job must accept another job that often pays less and requires fewer skills
4) his teachings are written in the Koran
6) in addition to English, language spoken by Israelis

Word Bank
Arabic
French
Hebrew
Iraq
Judaism
mosque
Muhammad
Ramadan
underemployment
Tehran

North Africa and the Middle East Economy

Directions: Read each sentence. Write *T* if the statement is *true* or *F* if it is *false*.

_____ 1) Most people in the Middle East and North Africa work in service industries.

_____ 2) Farmers in the deserts irrigate the land to grow crops.

_____ 3) Olives, grapes, oranges, and cork are the main crops grown in the Nile River Delta.

_____ 4) Rice and cotton are crops grown along the Mediterranean coast.

_____ 5) Saudi Arabia has one-fourth of the world's known deposits of oil.

_____ 6) The countries of the Middle East and North Africa have a lot of economic power because world industries depend on their oil for energy.

_____ 7) OPEC was founded in 1960 by countries who purchase oil from the Middle East.

_____ 8) OPEC tries to control the supply of oil by setting production limits.

_____ 9) Money from the sale of oil helps countries in North Africa and the Middle East build roads, housing, and schools.

_____ 10) Phosphates are a chief energy source in Morocco.

_____ 11) The Sahara and Nile Delta have large natural gas fields.

_____ 12) The United States is the Middle East's largest oil customer.

_____ 13) The Aswan Dam has both helped and harmed Egypt.

_____ 14) The level of pollution in the Nile is rising because the water flows more quickly.

_____ 15) The buildup of salt in the soil makes land useless for farming.

Getting to Know China

Directions: Complete the paragraphs. Write a word on each line.

China, the **1)** _____ largest country in area in the world, is located at about the same latitudes as the United States. It is bordered by **2)** _____ and Mongolia to the north. Vietnam, Laos, Myanmar, India, Bhutan, and **3)** _____ lie to the south. The East and South China Seas and the **4)** _____ are to the east. West of China lie India, Kazakhstan, Kyrgyzstan, Tajikistan, **5)** _____, and **6)** _____.

The rich farmland and good water supply in the **7)** _____ region were necessary for civilization to develop. China's natural borders have isolated and protected its people from foreign invaders for thousands of years. The Chinese also built a huge wall to keep invaders out. It is called the **8)** _____ and its main part is over 2,000 miles long.

China is a geographically diverse nation, with four main regions. The **9)** _____ is northeast of the capital city of **10)** _____. Most of the people who live here are **11)** _____. North of this area is the Manchurian Plain, which is the leading **12)** _____ area of China. Mountains and high **13)** _____ make up China's third region. Few people live in this region because of its harsh climate and geography. **14)** _____ and steppes make up China's fourth region. Farming here is difficult due to lack of rain, but nomadic Mongols and **15)** _____ have raised goats and sheep in this area for many years.

Make It True

Directions: Read each sentence. Write *T* if the statement is *true* or *F* if it is *false*. Make each false statement true by changing the underlined word(s). Write the correct word(s) on the line.

_____ 1) China is located at about the same latitude as <u>Canada</u>. _____

_____ 2) Huang means "<u>river</u>" in Chinese. _____

_____ 3) China is the <u>third</u> largest country in area in the world. _____

_____ 4) The Great Wall was built to keep <u>invaders</u> out of China. _____

_____ 5) Civilization first developed in the <u>Gobi Desert</u>. _____

_____ 6) China has <u>four</u> main geographical regions. _____

_____ 7) India and Pakistan border China to the <u>east</u>. _____

_____ 8) Loess is a fertile soil that was deposited on the plains of China by the <u>wind</u>.

_____

_____ 9) China's <u>deserts</u> are rich in mineral resources. _____

_____ 10) The <u>North China Plain</u> is the leading industrial area of China. _____

_____ 11) The <u>Qinghai-Tibet</u> Plateau is called "the roof of the world." _____

_____ 12) <u>Beijing</u> is the capital of China. _____

_____ 13) One-third of China is covered by <u>mountains</u>. _____

_____ 14) The <u>Manchurian Plain</u> is rich in coal and iron deposits. _____

_____ 15) Nomadic peoples raise sheep and goats in the <u>desert</u> regions of China.

_____

Understanding the Geography and Climate

Directions: Write the answers to these questions using complete sentences.

1) How does geography affect the kinds of houses people in China live in?

_____

_____

2) How does the climate affect what people in China eat?

_____

3) How were the Himalayas formed?

_____

4) Why do most Chinese people live on the plains of eastern China?

_____

5) Why is the Huang He called "China's Sorrow"?

_____

6) What is a floodplain?

_____

7) What is the climate of the Qinghai-Tibet Plateau like?

_____

8) Why is the Yangtze River important?

_____

_____

9) Why are farmers able to raise two crops a year in southern China?

_____

10) Why do farmers in Asia build terraces?

_____

_____

Describing the People of China

Directions: Write the answers to these questions using complete sentences.

1) To what cultural group do most Chinese people belong?

_____

2) Has Tibet always been part of China? Explain.

_____

_____

3) What is filial piety?

_____

4) What is the main message of Confucius's teachings?

_____

_____

5) Who was Siddhartha Gautama?

_____

_____

6) How is written Chinese different from written English?

_____

7) What is the "one child" rule?

_____

8) What are the living conditions like for most Chinese families in big cities?

_____

9) How does China's large population growth affect the Chinese people?

_____

10) What might happen if China took over Taiwan by force?

_____

Economy and Environment Puzzler

Directions: Write the correct word(s) from the Word Bank to complete the sentences.

Word Bank

deforestation	water table	Communists	tax break	textiles
coal	Beijing	hydroelectric	reform	Chongqing

1) Using water to create _____ power is an underdeveloped resource in China.

2) Acid rain is a serious problem in _____.

3) _____ provides over 70 percent of China's energy needs.

4) In 1949, the _____ took over China.

5) _____ has some of the worst air quality in the world.

6) _____ causes soil erosion, which reduces the amount of land on which farmers can raise crops.

7) China is the world's leading producer of _____.

8) The level at which underground water can be reached is called the _____.

9) In 1976, Chinese leaders introduced a new plan for economic _____.

10) A _____ means that companies are allowed to pay less money to the government for taxes.

Use five of the words from the sentences to fill in the words in the puzzle. The letters in the boxes spell the name of one of China's staple crops.

11) [___] A ___ ___ ___   T ___ ___ ___ E

12) ___ [___] ___ N ___ ___ ___ ___ G

13) R [___] ___ ___ ___ ___

14) ___ [___] X ___ ___ E ___ ___

15) [___] E ___ ___ ___ L ___ S

Japan and the Koreas —True or False

Directions: Read each sentence. Write *T* if the statement is *true* or *F* if
it is *false*.

_____ 1) North and South Korea are located on the eastern edge of Asia.

_____ 2) Japan is separated from Korea by the Yellow Sea.

_____ 3) Japan is an island nation.

_____ 4) The islands of Japan are about as large as the United States.

_____ 5) Honshu is Japan's largest island.

_____ 6) About half of Japan's population lives on Kyushu.

_____ 7) The capital of Japan is Tokyo.

_____ 8) The smallest of Japan's four major islands is Hokkaido.

_____ 9) The Ryukyu Islands are southwest of Japan's four larger islands.

_____ 10) Africa and the Middle East are closer to Japan than Korea and China.

_____ 11) The Japanese, Chinese, and Korean cultures have many things in common.

_____ 12) For hundreds of years, shoguns fought for the control of Korea.

_____ 13) Japan was united by Tokugawa Ieyasu in 1867.

_____ 14) The Tokugawa family encouraged the Japanese to trade with and travel to
other countries.

_____ 15) The Tokugawa family ruled Japan for over 200 years.

Physical Features of Japan and the Koreas

Directions: Write the correct word(s) from the Word Bank to complete the sentences.

Word Bank				
Mt. Fuji	continental	Japanese Alps	tsunamis	Kanto Plain
Honshu	Pacific	crater	Yokohama	harmony
South Korea	mountains	seaweed	summer	Japan Current

1) The main physical feature of Japan and Korea is _____.

2) Underwater earth movements or volcanic eruptions cause _____.

3) The longest and highest mountain range in Japan is the _____.

4) _____ has not erupted in almost 300 years.

5) Japan's most famous landmark is on the _____ coast of Honshu.

6) The _____ is an important farming and industrial center on Honshu.

7) _____ is an important Japanese seaport.

8) Most of Japan's people live on a narrow coastal plain on _____.

9) Mt. Sorak is the most famous mountain in _____.

10) A bowl-shaped opening at the mouth of a volcano is called a _____.

11) The Japanese add _____ to their food for flavor and protein.

12) Northern Japan has a humid _____ climate.

13) The _____ helps keep temperatures mild along Japan's coastal plain.

14) Over half of Korea's rain falls during _____.

15) _____, the ability to work together and blend in, is important to the Japanese.

Japan and the Koreas—Sentence Completion

Directions: Circle the word(s) in parentheses that best complete(s) each sentence.

1) Korea and Japan are located where (the mountains meet the ocean, several tectonic plates meet).

2) Japan has about 1,500 (tsunamis, earthquakes) each year.

3) The Japanese Alps run (down the length, across the width) of Honshu.

4) The last time Mt. Fuji erupted was in (1707, 1997).

5) Almost all of Japan's people live (in the mountains, on a narrow coastal plain).

6) (Kyoto, Tokyo) is the capital of Japan.

7) The cities of Osaka and Kobe are located on the (Kinki Plain, Kanto Plain).

8) About 70 percent of Korea is (covered by mountains, a desert).

9) Mt. Kumag is the most famous mountain in (North Korea, South Korea).

10) Today, the Japanese and the Koreans use their rivers mainly for (crop irrigation and hydroelectric power, transportation).

11) The Five Fuji lakes in Japan were formed when (snow melted and ran down from the mountains, volcanic material dammed a river).

12) Japan is one of the world's leading (forestry, fishing) nations.

13) The four main islands of Japan have (the same climate, different climates).

14) Parts of southern Korea have an almost (humid continental, subtropical) climate.

15) Because Japan has so many mountains, its people live on about (20 percent, 80 percent) of the land.

Crossword Puzzle About Japan and the Koreas

Directions: Read each clue. Choose a word from the Word Bank to complete the puzzle.

Across

2) play that presents history and legend with music, dance, and a chorus
6) physical work that requires little skill
8) ancient Japanese religion in which followers worship spirits in nature
10) change in this kind of balance is a big problem for Japan

Down

1) original people of Japan
3) society in which the people are pretty much the same
4) Korea's biggest problem is this kind
5) play that uses colorful costumes and makeup and exaggerated movements
7) belief that when people die, their souls are reborn into another living form
9) most Koreans are Buddhist, about 25 percent are this

Word Bank
kabuki
population
Shintoism
political
manual labor
reincarnation
homogeneous
Christian
Ainu
Noh

Economy and Environment Match

Directions: Match the words on the left with the correct description
on the right. Write the correct letter on the line.

_____ **1)** United States

_____ **2)** export economy

_____ **3)** robotics

_____ **4)** automobiles

_____ **5)** Taiwan

_____ **6)** nuclear power

_____ **7)** natural resources

_____ **8)** Pyongyang

_____ **9)** industrial growth

_____ **10)** garbage

_____ **11)** oil

_____ **12)** pollution

_____ **13)** service industries

_____ **14)** consumer electronics

_____ **15)** Akio Morita

a. technology of using machines to do factory work

b. capital of North Korea

c. developed to reduce Japan's need for imported oil

d. country with low labor costs that has attracted Japanese industry

e. cause of air and water pollution in Japan

f. every person in Japan throws away over 2.2 pounds of this a day

g. Japanese government has spent billions of dollars to reduce this

h. only country with a stronger economy than Japan

i. employ almost 60 percent of Japanese people

j. 25 percent of these sold in the U.S. are made in Japan

k. Japan's most costly import

l. type of economy in which a country depends on exports for growth

m. Japan and Korea have few of these

n. founder of a global electronics company

o. electronic products that people use in their homes

South Asia Facts

Directions: Read each sentence. Write *T* if the statement is *true* or *F* if it is *false*.

_____ **1)** The South Asian peninsula is about one-third the size of the United States.

_____ **2)** Most of the South Asian subcontinent is located between the equator and the Tropic of Capricorn.

_____ **3)** The Himalayas were formed when two tectonic plates collided.

_____ **4)** The Himalayas are the highest mountains in the world.

_____ **5)** The Indian subcontinent is surrounded by the Indian Ocean.

_____ **6)** India shares borders with Afghanistan and Sri Lanka.

_____ **7)** Nepal and Bhutan are located in the Himalayas.

_____ **8)** Armies invaded South Asia through mountain passes.

_____ **9)** People have been living in the Indus River Valley for at least 4,500 years.

_____ **10)** There is little cultural diversity in South Asia.

_____ **11)** Pakistan lies between Afghanistan and India.

_____ **12)** The Indian subcontinent has a strategic location between the Middle East and Africa.

_____ **13)** The mountainous region of South Asia is densely populated.

_____ **14)** The Deccan Plateau is located north of the Indo-Gangetic Plain.

_____ **15)** The Thar separates India from Pakistan.

Sorting Out South Asia's Climates

Directions: The main characteristics of the Indian subcontinent climates are listed below. Match the characteristic with the climate it describes. Write the letters on the lines under the correct heading.

a. temperatures get cooler the higher a person travels

b. produces high seasonal rainfall in the coastal areas of India

c. hot and dry most of the year

d. snow covers the ground much of the year

e. strong winds bring cyclones and heavy rains

f. natural vegetation is grasses with a few trees

g. rain falls year-round, although most of it falls in the summer

h. differs from tropical climates in that there is a cooler season

i. temperatures are hot year-round and there is high seasonal rainfall

j. farming depends on irrigation

Highland climate	Tropical monsoon climate	Tropical savanna climate
_____	_____	_____
_____	_____	
	_____	

Humid subtropical climate	Steppe climate
_____	_____
_____	_____

Vocabulary Match-Up

Directions: Match the words on the right with the correct description on the left.
Write the correct letter on the line.

_____ **1)** A Hindu god who represents the preserving
face of God

_____ **2)** A Hindu who does not belong to any caste
and works with death, blood, leather, and dirt

_____ **3)** A small group within a large caste with
its own rules about social practices

_____ **4)** A religion that combines the Muslim belief in
one god with parts of Hinduism

_____ **5)** A Hindu god who represents the creative face
of God

_____ **6)** A religion whose followers worship many gods

_____ **7)** The belief that when a person dies, the person's
soul is reborn into another living form

_____ **8)** A Hindu social group

_____ **9)** Reaching the perfect state of mind and becoming
one with the eternal spirit

_____ **10)** Duty, or the way to act in life

_____ **11)** A Hindu god representing the destroying face of God

_____ **12)** One's future

_____ **13)** A religion that began as a protest against the caste system

_____ **14)** Conditions in which people lack one or more of the basic
things needed to live

_____ **15)** A follower of the Islamic religion

a. Jainism

b. caste

c. untouchable

d. reincarnation

e. Sikhism

f. dharma

g. Muslim

h. nirvana

i. poverty

j. Shiva

k. Vishnu

l. Brahma

m. Hinduism

n. jati

o. karma

Understanding the People of South Asia

Directions: Circle the letter of the correct answer.

1) People from the east and south are _____ than people in the north.
   a. wealthier
   b. shorter and darker
   c. more educated
   d. taller and lighter

2) _____ is the language of the Indian government and larger businesses.
   a. Hindi
   b. Urdu
   c. Dzongkha
   d. English

3) Hindus worship _____ main god(s).
   a. one
   b. two
   c. three
   d. twelve

4) _____ is the belief that when a person dies, his or her soul is reborn into another living form.
   a. Reincarnation
   b. Partitioning
   c. Dharma
   d. Nirvana

5) Hindus who do the dirtiest jobs and are looked down upon by other Hindus are called the _____.
   a. jatis
   b. outcasts
   c. under caste
   d. untouchables

6) The way people live their life determines their _____.
   a. caste
   b. dharma
   c. karma
   d. jati

7) The biggest problem South Asia faces is _____.
   a. poverty
   b. urbanization
   c. population growth
   d. civil unrest

8) The British _____ India in 1947, causing many problems due to religious differences.
   a. invaded
   b. Christianized
   c. partitioned
   d. decentralized

9) _____ respect all life and will not farm because they do not want to harm any living thing.
   a. Sikhs
   b. Jains
   c. Muslims
   d. Hindus

10) In the caste system, _____ belong to the highest caste.
   a. children
   b. politicians
   c. men
   d. priests

Finding the Right Words

Directions: Complete the paragraphs. Write a word on each line.

Most of the people in South Asia are **1)** _____. In **2)** _____ and

3) _____, more than 90 percent of the people make their living this way. Most of the

farmers are **4)** _____ farmers. They use simple tools and little machinery. Many of the

farmers depend on **5)** _____ rains to grow their crops. Farmers in

6) _____ receive little rain, so they use irrigation.

South Asia has many natural resources. **7)** _____ power provides a cheap

energy source. India has large deposits of **8)** _____ and iron ore. Offshore wells in the

Arabian Sea may provide future **9)** _____ production. **10)** _____

produces enough oil for itself and for export. **11)** _____ has few natural resources.

There are many different industries in India. It has all the raw materials for a modern

steel industry, including a long-lasting supply of **12)** _____ and coal. But many

of its steel mills are old and inefficient. In the 1980s, many new industries began producing

13) _____ products for sale in India and for export. Multinational corporations are

beginning to invest in India, which has helped **14)** _____ the standard of living.

15) _____ industries, in which people make products in their homes, are an

important part of the economy.

Two of South Asia's biggest environmental problems are **16)** _____ and

17) _____ pollution. **18)** _____ and Mumbai have unsafe levels of

poisonous gases in the air. Human and animal **19)** _____ ends up in the rivers,

causing bad pollution. Forests are being cut down to build power and irrigation dams. Deforestation

leads to **20)** _____. The Indian government wants to save the remaining forests and

plant new trees. However, it does not have the resources to do so.

Facts About Southeast Asia

Directions: Circle the word(s) in parentheses that best complete(s)
each sentence.

1) Mainland Southeast Asia borders (India and China, Japan and Korea).

2) (Myanmar, Malaysia) is located on the southern part of the Malay Peninsula.

3) The Southeast Asian countries of Indonesia, the Philippines, Brunei, and
Papua New Guinea are (islands, on the mainland).

4) Southeast Asia's (manufacturing centers, geographic location) makes it
an important region.

5) Southeast Asia is (rich in, lacking) mineral and agricultural resources.

6) Spices from the Spice Islands were valuable to Europeans because they
(kept food from spoiling, reduced cooking times).

7) Before 1946, (Spain, the United States) controlled the Philippines.

8) The diverse cultures of Southeast Asia are a result of its (location, weather).

9) (The Malays, Muslim traders) were the first group of people to migrate
to Southeast Asia.

10) Western ideas were introduced to Southeast Asia by
(Indian traders, Europeans).

Physical Features and Climates—True or False

Directions: Read each sentence. Write *T* if the statement is *true* or *F* if it is *false*.

_____ 1) The physical features of the mainland and islands of Southeast Asia are the same.

_____ 2) The southern parts of Cambodia and Laos are covered with mountains.

_____ 3) A few volcanic islands make up Southeast Asia.

_____ 4) The Irrawaddy, the Chao Phraya, the Mekong, and the Red are important rivers in Southeast Asia.

_____ 5) Modern highways and large railroads are the main forms of transportation in Southeast Asia.

_____ 6) Farmers in drier areas use river water to irrigate their crops.

_____ 7) Rangoon is a city on mainland Myanmar.

_____ 8) Many people in Southeast Asia fish for a living.

_____ 9) Temperatures are high throughout the year because this region lies far north of the equator.

_____ 10) The northern and southern parts of Southeast Asia receive different amounts of rainfall than places near the equator.

_____ 11) Typhoons destroy crops and homes on many island nations in Southeast Asia.

_____ 12) The windward sides of the mountains receive less rain.

_____ 13) Although Southeast Asia lies in the Tropics, snow covers some mountain peaks.

_____ 14) Homes on stilts protect people from floods and wild animals.

_____ 15) Many people in Southeast Asia live much like their ancestors did.

The People of Southeast Asia

Directions: Write the correct word(s) from the Word Bank to complete each sentence.

```
                              Word Bank
    Thais        dialects      poverty      Hinduism     family planning
    majority     Myanmar       Indonesia    Philippines  Malay
```

1) _____ has four large minority groups.

2) The _____ are the largest ethnic group in Thailand.

3) More than half of a group of people or things is called a _____.

4) All of the languages of island Southeast Asia are of _____ origin.

5) Over 500 _____ are spoken in Indonesia.

6) _____ is a popular religion in Bali and Lombok.

7) _____ has the fourth largest population in the world.

8) To limit population growth, most countries in Southeast Asia have introduced

   _____.

9) The biggest problem in Southeast Asia is _____.

10) Ethnic and religious differences have caused fights for independence in parts

    of Indonesia and the _____.

Economy and Environment Puzzle

Directions: Read each clue. Choose a word from the Word Bank to complete the puzzle.

Across

1) covers a rice paddy
3) practice encouraged by capitalism
7) reason for Singapore's wealth
8) keeps tribal peoples from following their traditional ways of life
9) leading producer of chromium, nickel, copper, and gold

Down

2) diet staple of more than half of the world's people
3) job of two-thirds of the people of Southeast Asia
4) this is poorly developed in most countries in Southeast Asia
5) chief exporter of rice
6) one of the world's busiest seaports

Word Bank

economy

Philippines

farmer

location

foreign
   investment

water

Thailand

Singapore

rice

deforestation

What Do You Know About the Pacific World?

Directions: Write the correct word(s) from the Word Bank to complete each sentence.

Word Bank

Sydney	meridian	foreign countries	Polynesia	Western Australia
Melanesia	equator	Indian Ocean	continent	New Caledonia

1) Earth is divided into northern and southern hemispheres at the _____.

2) A(n) _____ is an imaginary line that circles Earth and runs through the North and South Poles.

3) Australia is both a country and a _____.

4) The _____ lies to the west and south of Australia.

5) _____ is northeast of Australia and New Zealand.

6) _____ is the largest subregion of the Pacific Islands.

7) _____ is the largest state in Australia.

8) _____ is the only country in Melanesia that is not independent.

9) Many Polynesians are still governed by _____.

10) _____ is Australia's largest city.

Physical Features and Climate of the Pacific World

Directions: Write the answers to the questions using complete sentences.

1) What is the highest point in Australia?

_____

2) What gives Uluru its orange-red color?

_____

3) What is a reef?

_____

4) Why does New Zealand have many earthquakes and volcanoes?

_____

_____

5) How were the Pacific Islands formed?

_____

_____

6) What do the people of New Zealand use their short, fast-moving rivers for?

_____

7) When does winter occur in the Southern Hemisphere?

_____

8) What kind of climate does two-thirds of Australia have?

_____

9) Why is the southwest coast of South Island one of the wettest areas in the world?

_____

_____

10) Where do most people in New Zealand live?

_____

Is It True About the People of the Pacific World?

Directions: Read each sentence. Write *T* if the statement is *true* or *F* if it is *false*.

_____ 1) Europeans arrived in Australia before the Aborigines did.

_____ 2) The Aborigines' name for themselves is Kooris.

_____ 3) The Aborigines had no form of written language.

_____ 4) The first European settlers in Australia were from Spain.

_____ 5) Australia has one of the highest percentages of immigrants
in the world.

_____ 6) The Maori are the native people of New Zealand.

_____ 7) In 1840, the Maori signed a treaty with the British government
that made New Zealand an independent country.

_____ 8) Although many Aborigines follow their ancient religion, some are Christians.

_____ 9) Christianity is a religion built around an idea called dreamtime.

_____ 10) Some Aboriginal words have become part of Australian English.

_____ 11) The population of the Pacific World is getting younger and growing.

_____ 12) Immigrants from Asia and the Middle East tend to have larger families, which
contribute to population growth in this region.

_____ 13) Most Australians and New Zealanders live in small rural villages.

_____ 14) New Zealand is not a member of the Commonwealth of Nations.

_____ 15) Both New Zealand and Australia have passed laws regarding the rights
of native peoples.

The Pacific World's Economy and Environment

Directions: Use the word(s) to write a sentence about the economy
and environment of the Pacific World.

agriculture   **1)** _____

_____

tourism   **2)** _____

_____

export   **3)** _____

_____

natural resources   **4)** _____

_____

trade   **5)** _____

_____

industries   **6)** _____

_____

marsupials   **7)** _____

_____

koalas   **8)** _____

_____

overgrazing   **9)** _____

_____

Great Barrier Reef   **10)** _____

_____

Geography Today

Directions: Read each sentence. Choose the word(s) from the Word
Bank that complete(s) each sentence.

Word Bank				
global village	interdependent	telecommunications	technology	satellites
computers	communication	Internet	transportation	e-mail

1) _____ can help geographers discover trends and patterns and solve hard math problems.

2) All the countries in the world are _____ because what happens in one country affects every other country.

3) _____ take pictures of Earth from space that help scientists track storms and check pollution.

4) Satellites, computers, cellular phones, and high-speed trains are all examples

   of modern _____.

5) The term _____ describes the sharing of ideas, cultures, and traditions around the world.

6) Changes in _____ have made the world seem smaller by making it easier for more people to travel around the world.

7) The Internet and e-mail are examples of _____.

8) The _____ is a large computer network that connects millions of people around the world.

9) Better _____ and transportation improve ways of collecting and studying information.

10) _____ allows people to send written messages around the world electronically.

Short Answers to Big Questions

Directions: Write the answers to these questions using complete sentences.

1) What do scientists think is causing global warming?

   _____

2) Why don't the ocean currents hold as much carbon dioxide as they used to?

   _____

3) What causes most air pollution?

   _____

4) What do scientists believe caused the hole in the ozone layer?

   _____

5) Why might the thinning of the ozone layer cause more skin cancer?

   _____

6) Where is water pollution most serious?

   _____

7) What causes soil erosion?

   _____

8) What do we call the ocean currents that are colder than usual?

   _____

9) What is it called when we adjust our clocks to make better use of daylight?

   _____

10) Who do developing countries depend on for money needed to clean up the environment?

   _____

11) What do we call countries that have already built their economies?

   _____

12) How does reducing the use of fossil fuels in developed countries hurt the economies of developing countries?

   _____

13) How can we reduce the amount of trash that ends up in landfills?

   _____

14) About how often does El Niño occur?

   _____

15) Give an example of people adapting to their environment.

   _____

The True Condition of Human Geography

Directions: Read each sentence. Write *T* if the statement is *true* or *F* if it is *false*. Make each false statement true by changing the underlined word(s). Write the correct word(s) on the line.

_____ 1) As the world becomes a global village, different cultures have <u>less</u> contact with one another. _____

_____ 2) The influence of the United States on the rest of the world has <u>lessened</u> since the end of World War II. _____

_____ 3) <u>English</u> is the official language of more than 75 countries. _____

_____ 4) AIDS <u>does not</u> affect people in Africa. _____

_____ 5) There are <u>more</u> poor people today than there were 25 years ago.

_____

_____ 6) <u>Developed</u> countries are most affected by war, poverty, disease, and overpopulation. _____

_____ 7) The <u>religion</u> of Latin America has influenced American popular culture.

_____

_____ 8) The new century promises a high standard of living for <u>most</u> people.

_____

_____ 9) <u>Individuals</u> make up the more than 25,000 international NGOs.

_____

_____ 10) The Economic and Social Council tries to improve the way people <u>communicate</u>.

_____

_____ 11) The United States <u>is</u> a member of the UN. _____

_____ 12) The International Court of <u>Disputes</u> tries to settle arguments between countries.

_____

_____ 13) In some countries, <u>children</u> must work because their families are so poor.

_____

_____ 14) People in developing countries live in <u>poor</u> housing. _____

_____ 15) The UN is <u>not always</u> successful in solving problems. _____

Sorting Out the Global Economy

Directions: Complete each statement by writing the missing word(s) on the lines.
Then use 13 of the letters in parentheses to spell a word for number 15
that describes a trend in the global economy. The numbers under the lines
tell which statement that letter comes from.

1) Developed countries send money to developing countries through the __ __ __ __ __ __

   (__) __ __ __.

2) Most people in __ __ __ __ (__) __ __ __ __ countries are highly skilled.

3) Both developing and developed countries __ __ __ (__) __ __ goods from other countries.

4) Developing countries often have the highest __ __ __ __ __ __ __ (__) __ __.

5) Most people in developed countries have __ __ __ __ (__) __ __ jobs.

6) Farmers __ __ (__) __ __ __ __ to large cities to find better jobs and a better life.

7) __ __ __ __ - (__) __ __ __ __ agreements allow countries to trade without barriers.

8) Because countries import many goods, they are able to __ __ __ __ __ __ __ __ (__) __
   in certain areas of production.

9) Farmers in developing countries have trouble getting their crops to market because of poor

   __ __ __ (__) __ __ __ __ __ __ __ __ __ __.

10) The population in less developed countries __ __ __ (__) __ __ __ every 25 years.

11) __ __ __ __ __ __ __ __ __ __ __ __ __ __ (__) trade has both an upside and a downside.

12) Money, medicine, tools, or machinery given by one country to help another country

   is called __ __ __ __ __ __ __ __   __ (__) __.

13) The __ __ (__) oversees trade agreements and provides help and training for
    developing countries.

14) Farmers in developed countries use a lot of __ (__) __ __ __ __ __ __ __.

15) ____ ____ ____ ____ ____ ____ ____ ____ ____ ____ ____ ____ ____ ____
     (6)   (2)   (13)   (1)   (14) (11)   (5)   (8)   (4)   (7)   (12)   (3)   (9)